STEMscopes™

TEXAS

STEMscopedia – 2, English
ISBN: **978-1-63037-008-4**

To learn more, visit us at www.acceleratelearning.com

3rd Printing 2015

TABLE OF CONTENTS

Accelerate Learning™

What is the difference between snow and water? Think about holding a snowball. A snowball feels cold. It is solid to the touch. You can change its shape by squishing it in your hands.

Water is a bit different than the snowball. Water can be hot or cold. It feels wet. If you spill water on your desk, it will form a puddle.

We have seen how snow and liquid water are different. What are some things that are similar to snow? Can you think of other things that are similar to water? Why do scientists need to be able to compare things in this way?

Objects are made up of matter. *Matter* is anything that has mass and takes up space. Snow is matter. Water is matter. YOU are matter! In fact, everything on Earth is made up of matter.

Our senses give us information about matter. You can see some matter with your eyes and touch some matter with your fingers. We can use this information to classify matter. When we *classify* things, we group them based on their similarities and differences.

Matter has physical properties we can describe. *Properties* include how something looks, feels, sounds, tastes, and smells. We have already described some properties of snowballs and water. Snowballs are cold and solid. Water is wet and can pour easily. It can be different temperatures.

We classify things based on their physical properties.

CLASSIFYING MATTER

Let's review more properties of matter.

- **Shape:** Objects have different shapes. For example, a notebook is shaped like a rectangle. A baseball is shaped like a circle. In the box below each picture, name the shape of each object. HINT: Use the words CIRCLE, SQUARE, or TRIANGLE.

A pyramid is shaped like a

_____ .

A globe is shaped like a

_____ .

A cube is shaped like a

_____ .

- **Mass:** The amount of matter in an object is its *mass*. If an object has a lot of mass, it is usually heavy. If an object has little mass, it is usually light.

what do you think •

A bowling ball and a balloon are about the same size and shape. Which object has more mass? Think about how easy they are to pick up. The bowling ball feels heavier, right? It has more mass than the balloon.

- **Temperature**: *Temperature* measures how hot or cold something is. An object's temperature can change. The temperature of the air outside changes with the seasons. When does it feel cold? When does it feel hot?

Lava is hot.

Snow is cold.

- **Texture:** *Texture* is what an object feels like. Sandpaper has a rough texture. Glass has a smooth texture. A cotton shirt is soft, while a rock is hard.

- **Flexibility:** *Flexible* objects bend easily. Some flexible objects will bend and stay that way. Other objects can return to their original shape.

We can use physical properties to classify matter.
Remember that classifying means grouping objects together based on their properties. Think about chocolate. There are different types of chocolate. Chocolate can be sweet or bitter. It can be solid or liquid. It can be light or dark. Those are all properties we use to describe, or talk about, different types of chocolate.

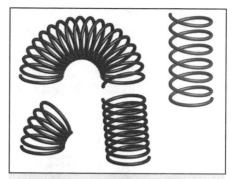

These springs are flexible. They bend and return to their original shape.

We classify these chocolates as solids. Some are light and some are dark.

We can classify chocolate milk with other liquids. Like water, it is wet.

We can classify matter as a solid or liquid based on its properties.
A *solid* object keeps its shape. This is a property. A *liquid* takes the shape of its container. That is another property.

Some objects can change from a solid to a liquid. When an ice cube becomes hot, it *melts*. The solid ice becomes liquid water. Objects can also change from a liquid to a solid. When water becomes cold, it *freezes*. The liquid water becomes solid ice. The properties of the water changes. It looks and feels different.

Accelerate Learning™

CLASSIFYING MATTER

Scientists classify objects to make it easier to study them. For example, different types of rocks have different properties. Astronauts found rocks on the Moon. These rocks were dark and had lots of holes. Scientists used these properties to classify the rocks as basalt. Basalt is made from cooled lava. This observation told scientists that lava once flowed on the Moon. The basalt was evidence that there used to be volcanoes on the Moon.

Everyday Life: What's to drink?

Classification is useful in everyday life, too. When you are thirsty, you want something to drink. But what would you choose? There are different types of drinks. Soda is sweet. Juice is also sweet, but it has more **nutrients**. Water and milk are not sweet. Water is clear. Milk is white.

> **nutrients:** things that keep you healthy

All of these liquids have different properties. Their different properties help you decide what to drink when you are thirsty. You can identify the type of liquid you want to drink based on those properties.

try now •

Can you classify your stuff? Take three objects out of your desk or backpack. Describe each object's properties. In other words, what does it look like? What does it feel like? Does it make noise or have a smell? Finally, name one object with similar properties. Write your answers in the table below.

What is the object?	What are its properties?	What object is similar?

CLASSIFYING MATTER

What Do You Know?

Can you classify the objects below? Write two to three words to describe the object in each box. The first has been done for you.

Snowball	Solid Round Cold Grainy
Barbell	Solid or liquid? Heavy or light? Is it flexible? Describe one more property:
Coffee	Solid or liquid? What is its color? Cold or hot? Describe one more property:

Classifying Matter

Children learn to classify objects at an early age. As they grow older and their vocabulary expands, their classifications become more complex and refined.

Take a trip with your child to a local natural history or science museum with a dinosaur exhibit. Start by reviewing a map of the museum with your child. Discuss the different classifications of artifacts in the museum, using the map as a reference. You might ask:

- Why are the dinosaurs in a different area from the other animals? *(They have different properties. They look different or have different body parts than other animals in the museum.)*

Walk to the dinosaur area of the museum. While viewing the dinosaur exhibits with your child, ask questions about the relationship between physical properties and the process of classification. For example:

- Did all dinosaurs move around the same way? *(Some dinosaurs flew, while others walked.)*

- Looking at the dinosaurs in the exhibit, which dinosaurs can be classified as "walkers" and "fliers"? What characteristics are used to make this classification? *("Walkers" have legs, while "fliers" have wings.)*

The previous exercise reinforced the idea of classifying objects based on their physical appearances and uses. Next, reinforce the concept of the physical properties of matter by finding a "touch and feel" or "fossil dig" area of the museum. If the museum lacks a hands-on fossil activity area, find a dinosaur fossil that is relatively close for observation. (Don't touch the fossil unless the museum allows you to.) Discussion questions may include:

- What are the physical properties of the fossil? *(Answers may include solid, smooth, or rough texture; descriptions of the fossil's shape; etc.)*

• •

Sometimes you feel too hot. Sometimes you feel too cold. How do you cool off? How do you warm up?

The fire gives the boys heat.

The fan cools the man.

Take another look at these pictures. How does the fire change the wood? How does the fire change the food? How else can heat change things?

Adding heat causes melting and evaporation. What happens if you add heat to ice? The ice *melts*. It changes from solid to liquid.

What happens if you add heat to water? The water boils. Eventually, it evaporates. When water evaporates, it changes from a liquid to a gas. The gas rises into the air.

Heat melts ice cubes. The solid ice changes to liquid water.

This was a lake. Heat caused the water to evaporate. As the water became gas, the lake dried up.

• •

Accelerate
Learning™

CHANGES FROM HEAT

Adding heat changes texture. *Texture* is how rough or smooth something feels. Ice may be bumpy or rough. Adding heat melts the edges and creates smooth water. Evaporation can change a lake bottom from smooth mud to rough, cracked soil.

what do you think •

Heat changes things in other ways. How did heat change these things? Fill in the blanks with these words: COLOR, SIZE, or SHAPE.

The burner changed

_____ .

The popcorn changed

_____ .

The candy changed

_____ .

look out! •

When we cool something, we take away heat. Water freezes when heat is removed. Freezing does not add cold.

Cooling changes things. Taking away heat *freezes* liquids. When a liquid freezes, it becomes a solid. Freezing gives liquids a shape.

How else can cooling change things? Red-hot objects are not red after they cool. Removing heat from smooth water can make ice cubes with rough edges. That means cooling something can change its shape and texture.

Cream mixed with sugar is runny. It turns into solid ice cream when it cools.

The man is making a horseshoe. It will turn black when it cools.

what do you think

Hot lava flows out of volcanoes. As it flows, it cools.

This picture shows both hot and cool lava. Write COOL next to the arrow pointing to the cool lava. Write HOT next to the arrow pointing to the hot lava.

Which property did you use to make your decision? Did color help you?

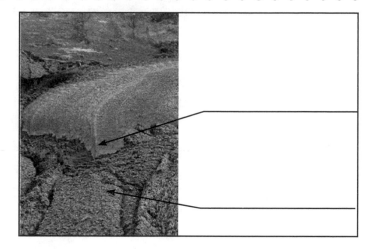

Discover Science: Changing Bridges

Metal things get bigger as they get hotter. They get smaller as they cool. A metal bridge has a different size and shape on a hot day than on a cool day. The people who design bridges must understand this. They add gaps around the metal pieces. Each piece has space to get bigger as it heats up.

This bridge changes shape as it heats up and cools down. Why isn't it damaged as it changes?

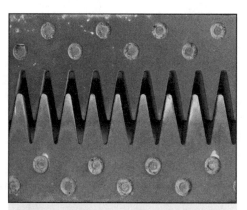

The bridge is made up of metal plates with gaps around them. As the plates get bigger, they fill the gaps.

CHANGES FROM HEAT

What Do You Know?

What happens to each object when you add or remove heat? Write your answers in the boxes beside the pictures. Use these words:

- Dry out
- Freeze
- Get shorter
- Melt

If you:		It will:
Add heat to ice cream		
Add heat to a wet towel		
Remove heat from a glass of water		
Remove heat from a metal rod		

CHANGES FROM HEAT

12

Heat and Air

In this investigation, you and your child will study the way that air can expand and contract when heat is added or removed. You will need these materials: an empty, plastic water or soda bottle (about one pint); a refrigerator freezer; and a hot water tap. The less rigid the bottle is, the better.

Begin by explaining that the empty bottle is not really empty because it is full of air. Explain that air is made of extremely small, moving particles. As these particles are heated, they move more quickly. As they are cooled, they slow down.

Follow this procedure to complete the investigation:

1. Put the cap on the bottle, and ask your child to squeeze it. Your child won't be able to crush the bottle because it is full of air.

2. With the cap still on, turn on the hot water tap and hold the bottle under it for one minute. Ask your child to try to squeeze the bottle again. It will be even harder to squeeze the bottle because the air inside expands when you add heat to it. (That is, the particles move more quickly and therefore farther apart.) For further proof, undo the cap and listen to the air rushing out.

3. Put the cap back on the bottle, and put the bottle in the freezer. Ask your child to predict what will happen to the bottle in the freezer.

4. Remove the bottle after 30 minutes, and ask your child to explain why it changed shape. (Air contracts when heat is removed. The particles slow down, and therefore they cannot move as far.)

5. Finally, have your child hold out his or her hands, palm up, and explain that you are going to pour cold air onto them. Remove the bottle cap and tip the bottle as you would when pouring water into someone's hands. Your child will feel the cold air on his or her palms. Explain that you were able to "pour" the air because cold air is heavier than warm air.

Here are some questions to discuss with your child:

1. Can you name something else that changes size when heat is added or removed?

2. What do you think would happen if we filled the bottle with water and put it in the freezer? (Explain that water, like air, is made up of extremely small, moving particles.) Although usually things shrink when they cool, water is unique in that the particles align to make a larger volume overall. This is more detail than you need to provide to your child, but you can discuss that water is different from other materials for that reason.

3. Hot air balloons are simply big balloons full of hot air. How did your experiment help

reflect •

Things often change. However, the materials they are made of might not change. We often make something new without creating a new material. These changes are called physical changes.

An iceberg was once many snowflakes. Snowflakes were once water. These things seem very different, but they are all made of water. A toothpick and a tree also seem different. Still, they are both made of wood.

Can you think of how things can change? What are some physical changes you have made to things?

Things can change in many ways. Here are some ways we change things.

Folding changes a flat piece of paper into an airplane.

Melting changes ice cubes into liquid water.

Cutting changes a tree into boards and sawdust.

How would you make these changes? Answer with these words:

• Sand   • Cut   • Freeze

To share a pie with friends:

_____

To change fruit juice into an ice pop:

_____

To smooth a piece of wood:

_____

PHYSICAL CHANGES

Everyday Life: Origami
Look at this picture. Can you see how the paper has been folded to make a swan? Folding paper to make shapes like animals is called *origami.*

Origami began in Japan, but people all over the world do it. You can find books at the library that show you how.

Different materials are used for different things. How do you choose which material to use for a project? Think about the material's **properties.** Ask yourself questions like these:

> **property:** how something looks, feels, sounds, smells, or tastes

• Do you need something hard?

• Do you need something you can cut?

• Do you need flexible materials? Something that is *flexible* can bend.

• Do you need materials you can burn?

Wood is good for building. It is sturdy yet easy to cut.

Glass is good for windows. You can see through it.

Plastic is a useful material. We can bend it into many shapes.

Metal is good for pots. It doesn't burn or melt easily.

try now

Open a drawer. It could be a kitchen drawer, a desk drawer, or a bathroom drawer. A "junk drawer" is good.

Make a list of the materials in the drawer. Your list will probably include wood, metal, plastic, and other materials. Count how many things are made of each material. Why do you think each thing is made of different materials?

A "junk drawer" contains many different things.

Your list of things may look like this:

What are things made of?	How many things are made of this?
Wood	3
Metal	6
Plastic	10
Rubber	3
Cloth	4
Other	5

what do you think

What materials would you use to make these objects? Choose materials that you found in your drawer, or choose other materials. If you want to, choose more than one material for each object.

Frying pan: _____

Shoelaces: _____

Button: _____

Spoon: _____

Accelerate Learning™

PHYSICAL CHANGES

Materials are often combined. Some things are made of more than one material. Many things wouldn't work very well if they were made of only one material.

Would you want a bicycle made only of metal?

Could a swing be made only of wood?

Some things would not work if they had missing parts. Shovels, hammers, and fly swatters would be useless without handles.

What Do You Know?
Cars are made of several different materials. Look at the picture of a car. Draw a line from the name of each material to a part of the car that is made of that material. (Different parts may contain the same material.)

Materials

• Metal

• Glass

• Rubber

What is it made of?

Choose a household item to disassemble and reassemble with your child. Your choice will depend on your available tools and your mechanical and technical abilities. The object you take apart could be as simple as a flashlight or a mechanical pencil or as complicated as a power tool or a small appliance.

A flashlight can serve as an example. Follow this procedure as you take it apart with your child:

1. Discuss each piece as you remove it from the flashlight. Ask your child to identify the material it is made of and to guess why that material was chosen. For example, the casing is likely plastic because it is sturdy yet inexpensive; the wires are copper because copper conducts electricity.

2. Stress the importance of arranging the parts in the order in which you removed them. This will help you to remember the order for reassembly.

3. Show how the different parts work together, and explain how removing a part would keep the flashlight from working properly.

4. Let your child try to reassemble the flashlight.

Here are some questions to discuss with your child:

1. What material(s) is each part made of? (A flashlight will include wires, a light bulb, a lens, a reflector, and an exterior casing.)

2. For each part, why was that material chosen?

3. For each part, would another material have worked as well?

Accelerate Learning™

reflect ●

When people talk about *energy*, what do they mean? Place a check mark next to each picture that you think shows energy.

When the power went out, I turned on a flashlight.

The butter melted when I heated it on the stove.

The crowd made so much noise that we could feel it.

look out! ●

Energy comes in many different forms. We will learn about three forms of energy: heat, light, and sound.

Heat is a form of energy. Have you ever seen a pot of water on a hot stove? First the pot gets hot. Then, the water gets hot. Adding heat energy to water makes it boil. What does water look like when it boils? You can see the effects of the heat energy.

The water is gaining heat energy. The heat causes the water to boil.

FORMS OF ENERGY

• •

Heat energy causes other changes. Adding heat energy to ice changes it to liquid water. This change is called *melting*. Think about ice cream on a hot day. The heat outside causes your ice cream to melt.

Heat makes most things larger. Blow up a balloon and tie it shut. Put the balloon in the freezer for one hour. The balloon loses heat energy in the freezer. How did the balloon change? Look at its size and shape. Now put the balloon in the hot sunlight. The balloon gains heat energy in the sunlight. How does the balloon change? Look again at its size and shape.

Sound is another form of energy. Sound energy happens when something moves quickly back and forth. This is called *vibrating*. We hear vibrations as sounds.

Different kinds of vibrations make different sounds. Some sounds have a high pitch. Fast vibrations cause the high-pitched sounds. Slow vibrations cause sounds with low pitches. Think about music—there are high and low sounds, right? These sounds are caused by different types of vibrations.

A plucked guitar string vibrates.

what do you think? •

We can produce sounds in many different ways. Look at the pictures of musical instruments.

- Which instrument do we blow on?
- Which instrument do we pound on?
- Which instrument do we pluck?

Harp

Trumpet

Drum

Accelerate Learning™

Scientists in the Spotlight: Amar Bose

Amar Bose is an expert on sound energy. He has used his knowledge to design better loudspeakers for playing music. Music sounds different in places like concert halls than in a car or our home. Each place makes music sound different. Bose's speakers make music from a home stereo or a car stereo sound like music at a live concert.

Light is another form of energy. The Sun produces light. Light is all so created from fires and things like light bulbs. We are able to see objects better when there is more light. That's because light bounces off things and goes to our eyes.

In bright light, we see more colors and details.

In dim light, we see fewer colors and details.

FORMS OF ENERGY

What Do You Know?
Here are some words related to energy.

• melt	• light energy
• The Sun	• heat energy
	• sound energy

Complete these sentences using the words in the box. You will use each word once.

1. Adding _____ can make water boil.

2. We hear music because of _____.

3. We see things because of _____.

4. Adding heat energy can make ice cream _____.

5. _____ is an important source of light energy that we see every day.

Sounds from a Vibrating String

All sounds originate from an object that is vibrating. The vibrations are usually difficult to see with the unaided eye. A plucked string is an exception. In this activity, you and your child will use a stretched rubber band as a vibrating string.

Begin by brainstorming about different types of sounds. Some sounds are high, and other sounds are low. This refers to a sound's pitch. Higher-pitched sounds come from more rapidly vibrating objects. Both the tension and length of the plucked string affect pitch. Some sounds are loud and others are soft. This refers to the amplitude. *Amplitude* is a measure of how far the object vibrates back and forth. In a stringed instrument, amplitude is controlled by how far back the center of the string is pulled when plucked.

For this activity, you will need a claw hammer; three nails; a short, wide board; and a large, strong rubber band. Help your child complete the following procedure:

1. Pound the nails into the board to form a triangle with unequal sides, like this:

The triangle should be about the same size as the maximum size to which the rubber band can be stretched.

2. Stretch the rubber band over the nails with equal tension on each side.
3. Pluck each side of the rubber band and observe the differences in pitch.
4. Pull hard on one side of the rubber band to increase the tension on the other two sides; observe the change in pitch of the two sides with increased tension.
5. Use a finger to hold the middle of the long side of the rubber band to the board; this will create two "new," shorter sections of rubber band on either side of your finger. Pluck each "new" section and observe its pitch.
6. Vary the distance you pull back on one of the sides of the rubber band when plucking. Observe the differences in loudness.

Here are some questions to discuss with your child:

1. Were you able to see differences in how fast the rubber band moved?
2. When was there a high sound? What about a low sound?
3. How far did each rubber band move? Did that make a difference?
4. What do you think affected how loud the sound was? Try plucking hard and then soft to find out.
5. How could you make a musical instrument using only the materials from this activity?

Accelerate
Learning™

What do you want to do with your artwork when you bring it home from school? You might hang it on the refrigerator. But what helps you do that?

People use magnets to hang paper on refrigerators. What is a magnet? How does it work?

Magnets help objects stick together. Magnets give off a special **force**. This force *attracts*, or pulls on, certain objects.

force: a push or pull

What this means is that some things stick to the magnet. But don't forget that magnets do not work on everything.

Magnets are attracted to many metals. Most refrigerator doors are metal. That's why magnets stick to metal doors. Magnets are especially attracted to the metals, iron and steel. Aluminum and copper are metals that do not stick to magnets.

An object that sticks to a magnet is *magnetic*. Iron nails, screws, and safety pins are magnetic. A non-magnetic object will not stick to a magnet. Wood and plastic objects are not magnetic.

These nails, pins, and paper clips are made of iron. They are magnetic.

Aluminum foil and copper pennies do not stick to magnets. Even though they are metals, they're not magnetic.

MAGNETS

Circle the magnetic object(s). Put an "X" over the non-magnetic object(s).

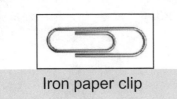

Iron paper clip

Copper penny

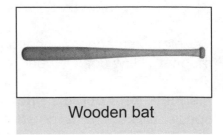

Wooden bat

Magnets create magnetic fields to attract objects. A magnetic field is an invisible force around the magnet.

Magnets have different ends. One end is called the south pole, and the other end is called the north pole.

Sometimes magnets attract each other. Other times, magnets push each other apart.

Magnets attract each other when their different poles are put together. Magnets push apart when the same poles are next to each other.

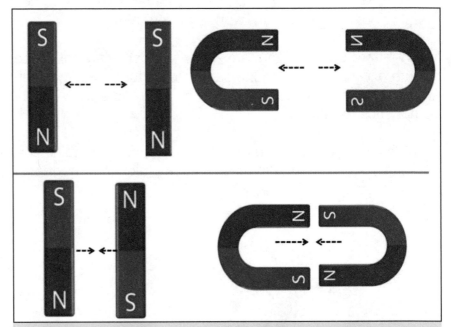

When north or south poles come together, magnets push apart. When opposite poles come together, magnets attract.

Accelerate Learning™

Magnets have different shapes and sizes. Some are shaped like horseshoes. Others look like sticks. Larger magnets are stronger than smaller magnets. A larger magnet can lift heavier objects.

We use small magnets to hold up notes.

We use medium-sized magnets in science labs.

Very large magnets can pick up cars.

try now •

Walk around your home with a magnet. Ask an adult to help. Place the magnet on different objects. Do not use the magnet near credit cards or computers. Below, make a list of objects that are magnetic and not magnetic. You can use words or pictures. Remember, a magnet sticks to magnetic objects and does not stick to non-magnetic objects.

Magnetic	Not magnetic

Accelerate Learning™

MAGNETS

Everyday Life: How do we use magnets?

Magnets are everywhere, even if you can't see them. Magnets help doorbells ring. They are in phones and speakers. They are in the motors of some cars.

We can turn some metals into magnets by running electricity through them. These powerful magnets are called *electromagnets*. We use electromagnets to move large objects like junk cars.

Magnets also help store information on credit cards. You should never place a magnet near a credit card. The magnet can erase the credit card information.

Even our planet is a big magnet! Earth has a north pole and a south pole. A compass is a tool with a magnet that points toward Earth's north pole. People use compasses to know which way is north.

Magnets power motors in electric cars.

Credit cards store data in magnetic strips.

The magnet in a compass always points north.

What Do You Know?

Magnets attract some objects but not others. Draw a line between the magnet and each object that WILL stick to the magnet. Put an "X" through the item that WILL NOT be attracted to a magnet.

Iron nails

Plastic cup

Steel fork

MAGNETS

Playing With Magnets

One way to help your child understand how magnets work is to create a magnetic "treasure chest." Find a clear plastic box about the size of a shoebox. Fill the box with uncooked rice and a dozen small magnetic objects. Magnetic objects include paper clips, small metal cars, and small metal washers. Do not add sharp objects, such as nails, safety pins, or needles. Add a dozen small, non-magnetic objects such as pennies, plastic toys, and crumpled pieces of aluminum foil.

Using a magnet strong enough to pick up the small magnetic objects, your child should dig through the rice using the magnet as the "treasure finder." Magnetic objects will stick to the magnet. As objects are found, remove them from the box to create a pile of "magnetic treasure." Non-magnetic objects should also be removed as they are found and added to a "junk pile."

As you search for magnetic treasure, you may wish to discuss the following questions with your child:

1. What types of objects will the magnet attract?
2. What types of objects will the magnet not attract?
3. What other magnetic and non-magnetic objects could you add to the box?

reflect

Think about going to a playground. Have you ever played on a slide? Where do you start? Where do you end up? Do you go in a straight line? Do you spin as you go?

These are all questions about *movement.* Can you think of some other ways that things move?

Things move from one place to another. The place where something is found is called its *position.* If something *moves,* it changes position. This change in position is also called *motion.*

There are many ways to move. These include rolling, sliding, and spinning.

- When something *rolls,* it turns over and over as it moves.
- When something *slides,* it moves along the surface of something.
- When something *spins,* it turns around and around a single point.

The rocks SLIDE down the hill.

Fill in the blanks about the other pictures.

HINT: Use ROLL or SPINS.

The top

_____

on a single point.

The balls

_____

up and down.

PATTERNS OF MOVEMENT

We can observe how things move. To *observe* is to see or look closely at something. In science, we don't just observe—we also think about our observations. We *describe* what we see, or tell others about it.

We can follow, or *trace,* the path of something moving. Based on what you see or observe, you can make predictions. When we *predict,* we say what we think will happen.

We observe that the snowball is rolling. It rolls down the hill.

We trace it turning over in its path.

We predict that the snowball will roll to the bottom of the hill.

We observe that the girl is spinning. She spins on one foot.

We trace her moving around and around.

We predict that she will keep spinning around.

We observe that the boy is sliding. He is not sliding in a straight line.

We trace him moving downhill. We trace the curves of his motion.

We predict that he will slide to the bottom of the hill.

Accelerate Learning™

PATTERNS OF MOVEMENT

The car in this picture is moving down the road.

What do you observe about the car?

The car is: (Circle the answer)

Sliding   Rolling   Spinning

Trace the motion of the car with your finger.

Describe the path you predict the car will take. Write your answer below.

_____

_____

_____

An object's properties affect its motion. *Properties* are things that we can see, feel, hear, smell, and touch. Some of an object's properties are size, shape, and weight.

look out!

A rock that is round can roll. A rock that is flat and smooth may slide, but it will probably not roll very well. A rock with a pointed end might be able to spin on the point. When we observe an object's properties, we can better predict its motion.

Discover Science: Newton's Laws of Motion

Sir Isaac Newton was a scientist. He observed the motion of many things. He described what he saw and shared this with others. He made predictions based on what he observed. He tested his predictions. Then he wrote three laws of motion. (In science, a *law* describes something that always happens.)

Accelerate Learning™

PATTERNS OF MOVEMENT

Here are Newton's three laws of motion:

1. An object that is moving will keep moving. An object that is not moving will keep not moving.

2. An object moves when something pushes or pulls it.

3. If one object pushes or pulls another object, the other object pushes or pulls back.

What Do You Know?
The sleds slide across the snow. As they slide, they make tracks. The red arrow traces the path of the red sled on the right.

Based on our observations, we can predict where each sled will go:

- The red sled will slide straight downhill.

- The blue sled will curve to the left as it slides downhill.

This picture shows a wind turbine with three blades. Describe your observations and make a prediction about the wind turbine.

Using your finger or a pencil, trace the path of the wind turbines blades. (The blades may move in either direction.)

The blades _____.

(HINT: ROLL, SPIN, or SLIDE)

What do you predict about the motion of the blades? Write your answer below.

_____

_____

_____

Accelerate Learning™

Moving Around the House

Discuss with your child the different kinds of motion they have learned about. These include rolling, spinning, and sliding. Challenge your child to demonstrate each kind of movement.

Then, walk through your home with your child and see how many items in motion you can find in each room. If you have an analog clock, for example, you might point out that the hands are spinning and have your child trace their movements. You may also point out a spinning ceiling fan.

After you have discussed any items that are already in motion in your home, select some objects to illustrate how the properties of an object affect its motion. For example, compare an orange and a banana. An orange is round and will roll. A banana will not roll; however, it can slide because it has a smooth surface, and it has points on which you can spin it. Find several examples of objects and talk with your child about the different ways each object can move.

Here are some questions to discuss with your child:

1. How do the physical properties of this object affect its motion?

2. How can you trace an object's movement from one place to another? What if the object is moving on a track? What if the object is not moving on a track?

3. How does moving help this object to *function,* or do its job?

reflect •

Cal and Jake play on the rocks. The river tumbles over them. Jake sits on a ledge. Water rushes over his legs. It splashes on his back. Cal laughs from a lower rock. Water tickles his toes.

Water has rushed over these rocks for a long time. It has made them smooth. Cal and Jake have to be careful. The rocks are slippery. They are cold.

property: how something looks, feels, sounds, tastes, or smells

You probably have some rocks where you live, too. With an adult, go outside and find some rocks. Choose a few rocks to observe. What are their **properties**? How can you describe them?

Rocks have different textures. *Texture* is how the surface of something feels. Does a rock feel smooth or rough? Is it soft or hard? Bumpy or sharp?

This rock is hard, rough, and bumpy.

Describe the textures of the rocks in the pictures below.

HINT: Use words like SMOOTH, ROUGH, and SHARP to help you.

The texture of this rock is

_____.

The texture of these rocks is

_____.

The texture of this rock is

_____.

ROCKS

Rocks are different colors. Look at the rocks around your school or home. What color are they?

Many rocks are brown, white, black, or gray.

People use red rocks to make garden paths around plants.

This piece of granite has speckles of different colors.

You can identify some rocks by their colors. The color *turquoise* is named for a blue-green stone. Look at the differently colored rocks below. Do their names have anything to do with their colors?

Blue Azurite   Clear Quartz   Turquoise

Speckled Granite   Brassy Pyrite   Red Sandstone

Some rocks have similar colors. Take a look at the picture of pyrite, above. Pyrite is sometimes called "fool's gold." Can you guess why?

Is this real gold or pyrite?

(It's real!)

Accelerate Learning™

ROCKS

Rocks are different sizes. You can estimate a rock's size. (When you *estimate,* you make an educated guess.) Simply compare the rock to your hands or feet.

This girl is sitting on a rock. It is bigger than her feet. Describe the rocks in the other pictures.

HINT: Use the words BIGGER or SMALLER in the blanks.

These rocks are

_____

than his fingers.

These rocks are

_____

than her hand.

This rock is

_____

than their arms.

try now

You can also measure the exact size of a rock. You will need a ruler to do this.

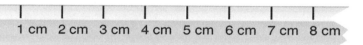

First, let's practice using these pictures of a ruler and a rock. The ruler is placed at one end of the rock. Look at the number at the other end of the rock, or count the tick marks. Here, each tick mark counts for 1 centimeter (cm). This rock is 6 cm wide.

Now, let's measure some actual rocks!

Accelerate Learning™

ROCKS

Career Corner: What does a geologist do?

Rocks have many uses. Many of our tools are made out of rocks. We grow plants in soil that contains rocks. Earth itself is made of rocks! It is important that we know as much as we can about rocks.

A *geologist* is a scientist who studies the physical parts of Earth. Some geologists study different types of rocks. If they find a rock, they might ask what it is made of. They might ask how the rock was made. Some geologists study animals or plants that become rocks after they die. These rocks are called *fossils*.

You have to go to college to become a geologist. Even if you decide not to focus on rocks, you will probably learn a lot about them. Rocks can be pretty interesting once we start looking more closely!

What Do You Know?

Take a few moments to study these rocks. Then, answer the questions about them.

Circle the best answer for each question.

What texture are these rocks?	Smooth all over
	Rough all over
	Partly smooth and partly rough
What color are these rocks?	Black all over
	White all over
	Mostly black with white spots
How wide is the smaller rock?	1 cm
	3 cm
	5 cm
	8 cm

ROCKS

Take a Rocky Scavenger Hunt

Children enjoy scavenger hunts, so take this opportunity to design your own treasure hunt with a "rocky" theme. One great way to do this and get some great exercise with your child is to take a hike together. Find a local hiking trail or hiking area where you will come across rocks. During the hike, ask your child to find rocks that have different textures, colors, and sizes.

For example, ask your child to find a smooth white rock. Then try to find a pebble as small as a fingertip, followed by a boulder larger than your foot. (Be careful about using terms such as *pebble* and *boulder*—at this level, some children may be confused by these categories. It's simpler to refer only to larger and smaller rocks.)

Here are some questions to discuss with your child:

1. Why are some rocks smooth and others rough?

2. Can you change the color of a rock? Why?

3. Why are some rocks tiny, whereas other rocks are as large as mountains?

4. What causes larger rocks to break into smaller pieces?

· ·

Emmy spent all day playing in the ocean. Heat from the Sun beat down on her. After a while, she noticed she was thirsty. She tried a sip of the ocean water. Yuk! It tasted terrible.

Emmy was surrounded by water. But she had to go somewhere else to find a drink. Why?

Some water is salt water. Earth's oceans are filled with salt water. So are the seas. Salt water has lots more salt than fresh water, which is why we can taste it.

Our bodies cannot handle that much salt. People cannot drink salt water at all. In fact, it will make us sick. That is why Emmy had to find a drink of fresh water instead of ocean water!

About three-fourths of Earth is covered in water. Almost all of this water is salt water. Remember that Earth's oceans and seas contain salt water. Some marshes also contain salt water. A *marsh* is an area along a coast filled with water and tall grasses.

About 97% of Earth's water is salt water. Most of this water is found in the oceans.

Many birds in salt marshes can drink salt water! When the birds drink the water, special glands remove the extra salt.

· ·

Accelerate Learning™

BODIES OF WATER

Some water is fresh water. Water that is not salt water is called *fresh water*. People and many animals cannot drink salt water. They must drink fresh water. Only 3% of all water on Earth is fresh water.

Most of Earth is covered in water. That is why our planet looks mostly blue. The blue areas are the big oceans!

We can drink only about 1% of the water on Earth. Where does this water come from? We cannot get it out of the ocean. Ocean water is too salty. We cannot get it from giant ice sheets, or *glaciers*. The water in glaciers is frozen.

Where can we find water that is both fresh and liquid? Here are some places. Write something you already know about these sources of fresh water:

Glaciers are huge sheets of ice.

• Streams:

_____

• Rivers:

_____

• Lakes:

_____

Accelerate Learning™

Let's learn more about these sources.

Streams are small bodies of water. They flow into rivers.

Rivers are wider and longer than streams. Many rivers flow from lakes to oceans.

Most lakes are completely surrounded by land. Some lakes connect to rivers.

Fresh water comes from other sources.
Rain water is fresh water. Fresh water also comes from underground lakes and streams. People can bring it up to the surface. They drill down into the ground. Then they build a well to bring up the water.

Rain provides fresh water. It runs off Earth's surface and fills rivers, streams, and lakes.

look out!

Not all lakes contain fresh water, though. Some lakes are full of salt water. China has many salt-water lakes. The United States has one of the most famous ones. Salt Lake City in Utah is named for the nearby Great Salt Lake.
The lake is saltier than Earth's oceans!

Salt collects on the shores of the Great Salt Lake in Utah. The lake gets very little rain. No rivers flow into it. Why would this make it salty?

Accelerate Learning™

BODIES OF WATER

What Do You Know?
Look at the following photographs. Decide whether they show fresh water or salt water.
Circle your answers.

Fresh water   Salt water

Fresh water   Salt water

Fresh water   Salt water

Career Corner: Oceanographer
Scientists who study Earth's oceans are called *oceanographers*. There are different kinds of oceanographers. They study different parts of the oceans.

Marine biologists are oceanographers. They study plants and animals that live in oceans. Oceanographers can also study **climate**. If Earth's climate becomes warmer, oceans will become warmer. This affects the plants and animals that live in and next to the oceans. Oceanographers may also study ocean waves. This is important because large waves can damage buildings and hurt people if they reach shore. Knowing how waves move can help save lives.

> **climate:** the weather in a place over many years

BODIES OF WATER

Water Body Postcards

This project can help your child to better appreciate local water bodies. First, visit one or more lakes, streams, oceans, or other water bodies near where you live. (You may also visit manmade water bodies such as reservoirs, though be sure to explain to your child that people created these particular water bodies to meet their need for fresh water or their desire for recreation.) If you do not live close enough to a water body to easily visit it, conduct online research on a nearby water body. Your child should be able to describe the water (fresh or salt), as well as the kinds of organisms that live in or around the water body. Encourage your child to learn how people in the community use the water body. If the water is fresh, do people drink it? Do people use it for bathing or cooking? If the water is salty, do people swim in it? Do they catch fish in it?

At home, instruct your child to make a postcard describing the water body for people who might want to visit it. The postcard should clearly identify whether the water body is a lake, stream, pond, or some other type of water body. Your child should include illustrations of the water body and of any organisms that live nearby. The illustrations should also show how people use the water body.

Here are some questions to discuss with your child:

1. How do people in our community use this water body?

2. Why is the water in this water body useful for these purposes?

3. Has our community had to address problems with the water body such as pollution or overuse? If so, how have we attempted to solve these problems?

reflect •

Look at the things around your classroom. What are they made of? Your books are made of paper. But where does paper come from? Paper is made from trees.

All the things in our life are made from resources. A *resource* is something that can be used. For example, trees are a resource. A tree's wood can be used to make paper for books.

There are many other resources. There are natural resources like trees. There are also manmade resources like books. Let's find out more about these two types of resources.

What resources do you see in this picture?

***Natural resources* are made by nature.** Some resources are made beneath the ground. Rocks and metals like aluminum are made under the ground. Other natural resources are made on Earth's surface. These include trees, plants, and soil. There are even natural resources above Earth's surface, like the wind.

People use natural resources in many ways. The pictures below show how we use some natural resources.

This house is made from mud. Mud is a natural resource made by mixing soil and water.

What natural resources do you see in the three pictures on the next page?

RESOURCES

Houses are made of many natural resources. In this picture, the main resource is

_____.

Soda cans are made from aluminum, a kind of

_____.

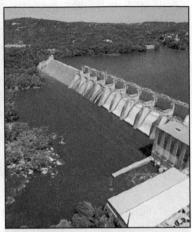

Electricity is made at this dam using flowing

_____.

Other kinds of resources are made by people. We call these resources *manmade*. Manmade resources do not come straight from Earth. Instead, people change natural resources to make new resources such as glass, plastic, and cloth.

Manmade resources are very useful. They often help us solve problems that natural resources aren't very good at solving. For example, glass is better than rock or metal for making a window.

Clothes are made from cloth. What else is made from cloth?

_____

_____

Many toys are made from plastic. What else is made from plastic?

_____

_____

Accelerate Learning™

You can't dig plastic out of the ground, but it still comes from Earth. You can't pick paper from trees, but it still comes from trees. People make manmade resources by changing natural resources.

How do people make paper from wood? Wood is a natural resource. People cut wood into tiny pieces and soak the pieces in water. When the wood pieces dry, they are smoothed with hot rollers. Machines squeeze and steam out the water. In this way, natural wood becomes manmade paper.

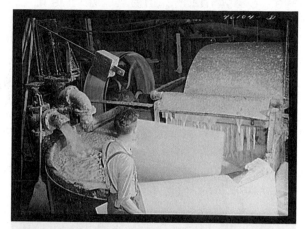

A paper maker soaks small pieces of wood in water.

Cotton comes from plants.

All manmade resources use materials from Earth. Glass is made up of grains of sand. Cloth fabrics come from many different natural resources.

Look at the labels on some of your clothes. Do you have clothes made of cotton? Wool? Silk? Each of these fabrics comes from a different natural resource. Don't forget they're all connected to natural resources!

Wool is made from sheep's hair.

Silk comes from tiny silkworms.

Accelerate Learning™

RESOURCES

Looking to the Future: Plastic for Dinner?

Plastic lasts a long time. When it is thrown away, it lasts for many years as trash. Now there is too much trash on Earth. How else can we get rid of plastic after we use it?

Like gasoline, most plastics are made from oil. They are not safe to eat. However, people are inventing new kinds of plastics that are safe to eat. They come in different flavors and melt in your mouth. Some even provide important things your body needs.

Plastics create a lot of trash.

Why might it be a good idea to make plastic that people can eat?

_____

_____

What Do You Know?

Wind is a natural resource that we use to make electricity.

For each resource listed on the next page, write if it is natural or manmade. Then describe one way you might have seen the resource used. You can be creative—there are many right answers! The first one has been done for you.

Wind causes this windmill to turn. As the windmill turns, it makes electricity.

Resource	Natural or manmade?	Where have you seen the resource used?
Rocks	natural	People use rocks to build walls.

Now you try!

Resource	Natural or manmade?	Where have you seen the resource used?
Bread		
Water		
Glass		

RESOURCES

Make a Manmade Resource

To help your child understand how people turn natural resources into manmade resources, make your own paper.

First, gather these materials:

- old newspapers or junk mail (no plastic pieces)
- a large aluminum pan
- warm water
- a hand beater
- a blender
- a piece of wire mesh with very small holes
- a towel
- a piece of cotton cloth such as a t-shirt

You will also need a smooth board for pressing the paper; a large cutting board from the kitchen will work well.

Tear up the old newspaper and junk mail into small pieces and place them in the aluminum pan. Cover the paper pieces with warm water and allow them to soak for 24 hours. The next day, drain as much of the water off as possible and add new warm water. Beat the water-paper mixture with a hand beater until it forms a soupy pulp. Then place the pulp into the blender, along with more warm water, and blend the mixture using short bursts. You want to break apart the pieces of pulp so that the individual paper fibers remain.

Prepare for the next step by placing the wire mesh on top of a towel. Once the pulp is broken down, pour it in a smooth layer over the wire mesh.

You can even have your child add flower petals or other small flat items to customize their paper. Use the smooth board to press on the top of the mesh to remove all the excess water. Finally, flip the screen onto the piece of cloth so that the paper separates from the screen onto the cloth. Allow the paper to dry until it can be used.

Here are some questions to discuss with your child:

1. Why are natural resources useful?

2. Which things in your home are made from natural resources? Which things are manmade resources?

3. What are the advantages of using a manmade resource rather than a natural resource? Are there any advantages of using a natural resource rather than a manmade resource?

4. How different is the paper you made from paper you might buy in a store? What do you think causes these differences?

• •

How would you describe the weather today? Is it hot or cold? It is clear or rainy? What do you need to know to describe the weather?

How has the weather affected your day? Did it cause you to wear certain clothing? Did the weather make you change your plans?

Weather describes what is happening in the atmosphere. The *atmosphere* is the layer of air around Earth. The air may be hot or cold.

Other things also affect weather. The air may be moving quickly. This is called *wind*. The sky may be full of clouds. Rain or snow may be falling from the clouds to the ground.

People use tools to learn about weather. A *tool* is anything that can gather information. Tools help us measure different things. This comes in handy when we want to find out more about the weather.

There are many kinds of weather tools. They gather different information about the weather.

- **Temperature:** *Temperature* is a measure of how hot or cold something is. A *thermometer* is a tool that measures temperature. Most scientists measure temperature in degrees Celsius. This is shown as °C.

  Suppose the air temperature is 32°C. You might say the weather is hot. Now suppose the temperature drops to 5°C. You might say the weather is cold. Higher temperatures mean the air is hotter.

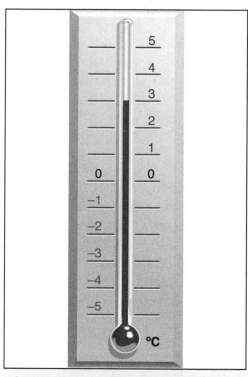

According to this thermometer, the temperature is about

_____ °C.
(HINT: What number is next to the top of the red line?)

Accelerate Learning™

WEATHER

- **Wind:** *Wind* is air that moves from place to place. Describing weather includes telling about wind. *Wind speed* is how fast the air moves. Air that moves slowly is called a breeze. A storm can have strong, fast winds.

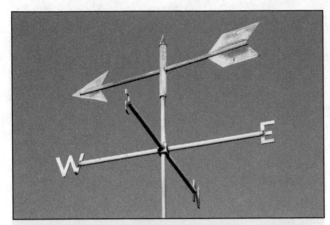

Wind turns a *weather vane*. The arrow points in the wind's direction. (W means west, and E means east. N means north, and S means south.)

A *wind sock* shows how fast the wind is going. It can show direction, too. The cloth tube fills up when the wind is strong. It flattens when there is no wind.

Getting Technical: Rain Gauge

One kind of weather tool is a *rain gauge*. This tool measures how much rain falls. It looks like a tube. Rain falls into it. Markings on the tube measure the height of the rain. The measurement is often in inches. It might also be in centimeters. You might say that two inches of rain fell.

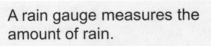

A rain gauge measures the amount of rain.

Accelerate Learning™

You can record weather data in different ways. The simplest way to record data is to write them down. You can organize some data in charts and tables. This makes the data easier to read. Charts and tables are useful for listing numbers.

For example, this table shows the high temperature on each day for a week.

Day	Sun.	Mon.	Tues.	Wed.	Thurs.	Fri.	Sat.
Temperature (°C)	32	34	33	36	37	35	34

Not all weather data are made up of numbers. Data can also be descriptions. You can describe the clouds in the sky. Are they white and fluffy? Or are the clouds dark and gray? Rain might be falling from clouds. Or the clouds could be making snow.

try now •

Make your own weather report.

1. Look or go outside.

2. Describe the weather. Include as many details as you can.

3. Compare your weather report with a friend's weather report.

4. Talk about why it is important to include details in your reports.

Weather information helps people make decisions. You might wear warm clothing if you know the weather will be cold. You might carry an umbrella if it is raining. You can dress properly if you know the weather. People also use weather information to decide what things they might do.

People may go swimming when it is hot.

People may go ice skating when it snows.

WEATHER

What Do You Know?
Draw a line to the tool that can answer each question.

How hot is it?

How much rain fell?

What direction is the wind blowing?

Rain gauge

Weather vane

Thermometer

Accelerate Learning™

• • • • • • • • • • • • • • • • • • •

Track the Weather

For this activity, you will need any type of outdoor thermometer. Place the thermometer in a place where you can read it easily and where it won't be disturbed for a period of time. You might place it on a deck railing or on a tree, for example. Try not to place it in direct sunlight because that will alter your measurements.

1. Before you begin the activity, your child should create a chart to collect weather data. It might be similar to the one below. Include enough rows for each observation your child will make.

   a. Your thermometer may have either the Fahrenheit scale (°F) or the Celsius scale (°C). (If you use the Fahrenheit scale, explain to your child that degrees Fahrenheit is the unit most commonly used in the United States to measure temperature.) Be sure to indicate the scale you use in your chart.

   b. If you have a weather vane or wind sock, use it to add details to your chart.

   c. Be sure to note any type of precipitation (e.g., rain, snow, sleet, or hail) that might be falling when you make your observations.

Date/Time	Temperature	Conditions

2. Your child should decide how often to record data. For example, you might collect data several times during the same day. Or you might collect data once a day for 10 days. Choose a schedule that works for you and your child, but try to include as many observations as you can.

3. As you prepare to make an observation, your child should record the date and time in the chart. If you are making measurements daily, try to make your observations at about the same time each day for consistency.

4. Your child should read the measurement on the thermometer and record the temperature in your chart.

5. Your child should observe the general conditions and write a description in the chart. For example, indicate if it is raining or snowing. Tell if it is cloudy or clear. Describe if there are light winds, strong winds, or no winds. Include any other weather details you can observe.

6. Your child should create a graph to show your temperature data, and add notes to the graph about the observations you made.

7. Analyze the graph with your child to look for any patterns or trends such as increasing or decreasing temperatures or winds. You may wish to consult weather data available in your local newspaper or on the Internet to compare it with your own.

Here are some questions to discuss with your child:

1. Did the temperature data show any trends? If so, what are they?

2. Were you able to predict the next day's weather based on the weather the day before?

3. Why do you think it is useful to know the weather conditions?

4. What might sudden changes in weather conditions mean?

5. How did tools help you to make observations? What other tools might help you add details to your chart?

6. How did the graph help you to analyze the data?

• •

You can find water in many places. It comes out of faucets in your house. It is also in lakes and rivers. The oceans are full of water. Rain is water that falls from the sky. Snow is frozen rain. Even clouds are made of water.

All of the water on Earth is *recycled*. That means that it gets used over and over again.

How do you think this water is recycled? Where does this recycling start? How does recycling water cause rain and snow?

Water moves through a cycle. A *cycle* is like a circle. It has no end and no beginning. The *water cycle* is how water moves around the world. The water cycle has three main steps.

Water on Earth moves in a circle through the water cycle.

Let's look at the main steps of the water cycle. The steps are numbered 1–3, but they are all happening at the same time on Earth in different places. Remember, a cycle has no beginning and no end.

- **Step 1: The Sun heats water on Earth.** Have you ever seen a puddle dry up after it rains? Sunlight heats the water in the puddle. When the water gets warm enough it moves into the air. This is called evaporation. You can't see water in the air. It is invisible.

Puddles disappear when their water moves into the air.

Accelerate Learning™

WATER CYCLE

Evaporation also happens in oceans, lakes, and rivers. The Sun warms the water. The water moves into the air.

try now •

There is a lot of water in oceans, lakes, and rivers. The Sun can dry up a whole puddle, but it doesn't dry up the whole ocean. Only some of the ocean water evaporates. A lake or river can dry up if there is no rain and it is very hot.

There used to be a river here before the Sun's heat dried it up.

- **Step 2: What happens after water moves into the air?** The water gets colder as it rises through the air. When it gets cold enough, it makes or forms clouds. This is called *condensation*. The water is not invisible anymore. Clouds might look like puffy cotton, but they are really made of very tiny drops of water. You cannot sit on a cloud. You would fall right through and get quite wet!

From far away clouds look like puffs of dry cotton.

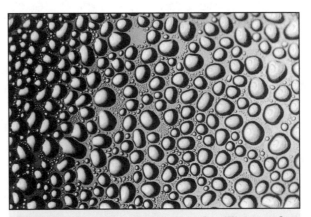

In fact, clouds are made of millions of tiny drops of water.

- **Step 3: What happens after clouds form?** As clouds fill up with water they become heavy. Clouds cannot float in the sky if they are too heavy. So the water drops in clouds begin to fall back to the ground. We call this falling water *precipitation*.

Accelerate Learning™

We call precipitation that falls as liquid water *rain*. Sometimes it is very cold when rain falls. The water turns into freezing rain or snow as it falls to the ground. Hail and sleet are other kinds of icy precipitation.

| Rain | Hail | Sleet | Snow |

When precipitation like rain reaches Earth, it flows back into rivers, lakes, and oceans. The Sun's heat evaporates the water, and the water cycle continues.

All the water on Earth moves through three main steps in the water cycle. Identify each step in the diagram below. Use these words to complete the blanks: CONDENSATION, EVAPORATION, and PRECIPITATION.

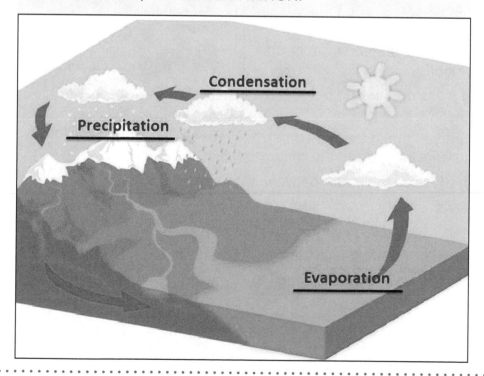

Accelerate Learning™

WATER CYCLE

The words in the box refer to different steps in the water cycle. Use these words to complete the sentences below.

Word Box

sunlight	never	ground
rivers	circle	cycle

Water falls to the _____ when it rains. The water flows across the ground into

oceans, _____, and lakes. Then the water _____ starts again at

Step 1. The _____ heats water. The water cycle _____ stops. It

keeps moving in a _____.

try now

Model the water cycle with five friends. Each person will play different parts of the water cycle.

1. Give each person a part. One person is an ocean. The other people are the Sun, the sky, a cloud, or the ground.

2. Stand in a circle. The Sun person stands outside the circle.

3. Make sure you are in the right order that water moves through the cycle.

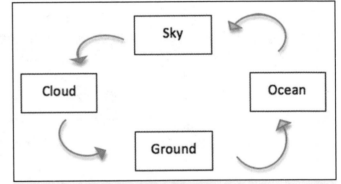

Stand in this order for Step 3.

4. The Sun will pass the water between the ocean and sky.

5. Each person should hold a large, empty cup.

6. The ocean person starts with a cup filled with water.

7. Pass the water around the circle by pouring it into each person's cup.

8. Continue moving the water through the cycle.

What's the Word: Cycle and Recycle

The word *cycle* means "circle" or "wheel." Water moves through the water cycle in a kind of circle.

Other words also use *cycle*. A bicycle has two wheels. A tricycle has three wheels. The prefix *re-* means "again." If you add *re-* to *cycle* you get *recycle*. So, *recycle* means to move in a circle again.

What Do You Know?

Look at the pictures below. Decide which step of the water cycle they show (1, 2, or 3). Then write a sentence that describes the picture including the words *evaporation, condensation,* or *precipitation.* The first one has been done to show you.

The word *bicycle* means "two wheels."

Picture	Which step in the water cycle?	What is happening?
	3	Rain is a kind of precipitation in the water cycle.

WATER CYCLE

Now you try! Here is a reminder to help you:
1 = Evaporation
2 = Condensation
3 = Precipitation

Picture	Which step in the water cycle?	What is happening?

The Water Cycle in 3-D

To help your child continue learning about the water cycle, work together to create a three-dimensional poster that models the processes involved in the water cycle. Build the model on a large piece of poster board and use a variety of materials to represent the different aspects of the water cycle. For example, you may use cotton balls as clouds; colored cling wrap as oceans, river, or lakes; plastic beads as raindrops; and magazine clippings or photographs for the Sun.

Start in the same place as the companion: the evaporation of oceans, rivers, and lakes (Step 1). Your child should then proceed to Steps 2 and 3, adding the appropriate parts to the poster board and labeling them. In addition, your child should write a description of each step on a small index card (e.g., evaporation, condensation, precipitation). Glue each index card to the poster board beside the correct step. Your child should draw arrows to show how water moves from step to step.

Here are some questions to discuss with your child:

1. Why is the water cycle called a cycle?
2. What are the major steps of the water cycle?
3. How does the water cycle cause weather conditions?

reflect •

Looking up to the sky, you can see many interesting things. You have probably seen the Moon many times. Sometimes you see it at night. Other times you can see it during the day.

You may have noticed that the Moon can look different. It can look like a circle. It can also look curved. Other times you can't see it at all. Why does the Moon seem to change?

The Moon is lit by the Sun. The Moon can look bright in the sky. But it does not make its own light. The Moon is bright because of the Sun. Light from the Sun shines on the Moon. The Sun lights up the side of the Moon facing the Sun. The side of the Moon facing away from the Sun is dark.

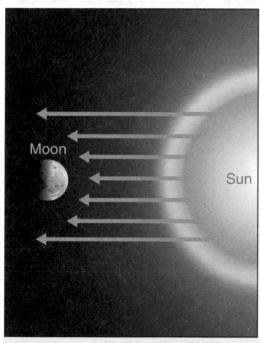

The Sun lights up half of the Moon.

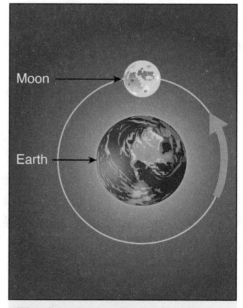

The Moon moves, or revolves, around Earth.

The Moon moves around Earth. The Moon travels around Earth in a path called an *orbit*. The Moon takes about 28 days to go all the way around Earth. That's about one month.

OBJECTS IN THE SKY

The Moon looks different during the month. You see the part of the Moon facing Earth. The amount of the lit side you can see changes as the Moon moves.

The Moon does not change as it moves around Earth.

However, you see different parts of the Moon as it moves.

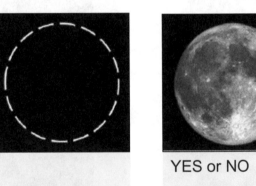

Look at these pictures. Can we see the Sun's light bouncing off the Moon? Circle YES or NO in each picture. What evidence did you use from the pictures?

YES or NO

Explain why you think so:

_____

_____

YES or NO

Explain why you think so:

_____

_____

Accelerate Learning™

try now

You can describe the different shapes of the Moon. Try looking for the Moon in the sky tonight. Draw its shape on a calendar. Draw the Moon every few days. Use words to describe how the Moon looks. HINT: You can try using words such as HALF, THREE-QUARTERS, FULL, and CRESCENT or SLIVER. You can also make up your own words to describe the shapes you see.

The Sun can look different, too. The Sun does not change. It can look different because of the way Earth moves. One way Earth moves is by spinning. Earth spins like a top. Another way to say this is that Earth *rotates*.

The way Earth spins causes day and night. Earth does not make its own light. It is lit by the Sun. One side of Earth faces the Sun. It is lit up and has daytime. The other side of Earth is dark. It has nighttime.

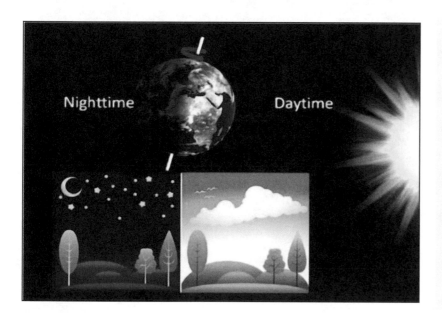

Draw arrows from the Sun to the part of Earth where it is daytime.

The arrows show how sunlight causes day and night.

look out!

The Sun looks like it rises and sets. The Sun appears to rise every morning. The Sun does not really move through the sky. It looks like it moves because of how Earth spins. Sunrise happens when a place on Earth spins into the Sun's light.

The Sun looks like it moves across the sky during the day. It seems to get higher in the sky for half of the day. It is highest at noon. Then it starts to get lower. The Sun sets when a place on Earth spins away from the Sun. It's Earth moving! The Sun doesn't move.

Accelerate Learning™

Getting Technical: Optical Telescope

People can use telescopes to learn about objects in space. A telescope makes faraway objects look closer. An optical telescope gathers light to help you see.

Modeling the Moon's Phases

Gather a flashlight or a lamp along with any kind of ball, such as a soccer ball or beach ball. You will also need a balloon, a marker, and a ruler. Inflate the balloon so that it is smaller than the ball.

1. Set up the lamp or flashlight on a table or floor, and turn it on. This represents the Sun.

2. Place the ball some distance from the light source. The ball represents Earth.

3. Have your child hold the balloon to represent the Moon.

4. Dim the lights in the room other than the flashlight or the lamp.

5. Observe the half of the balloon lit by the light source.

6. Use the marker to draw a line around the balloon that separates the light side from the dark side.

7. Ask your child to move the Moon around Earth. Direct your child to keep the lit half of the balloon always facing the light source.

8. Stop the balloon at different positions. Hold the ruler from Earth to the balloon. Observe how the portion of the lit half facing Earth varies.

Half of the Moon is always lit by the Sun. As the Moon revolves around Earth, observers on Earth can see different portions of the lit half. This causes the Moon to have a different appearance even though the Moon itself does not change. The different appearances of the Moon are known as *phases*. The Moon revolves around Earth once about every 28 days, so the cycle of phases takes 28 days.

Use the ruler to get an idea of the view from Earth. You should observe that when Earth is directly between the Moon and the Sun, observers on Earth can see all the lit half of the Moon. Your ruler should point directly from the ball to the center of the lit half of the balloon. This position represents a Full Moon.

When the Moon is directly between Earth and the Sun, observers on Earth can't see any of the lit half of the Moon. Your ruler should point directly from the ball to the center of the dark half of the balloon. This represents a New Moon.

Note that the opposite side of the balloon will not be in complete darkness. In a room, the light will spread out enough that the back of the balloon may be slightly lit. However, consider the brightly lit side of the balloon as the lit half and the opposite side as the dark half.

OBJECTS IN THE SKY

Here are some questions to discuss with your child:

1. Why does the Moon look like it lights up? How much is lit up at any time?

2. Why can't you see the Moon at all on some nights?

3. Does the size of the Moon change during its phases?

4. Would the Moon go through phases if it did not revolve around Earth? Explain.

reflect

Some people think they need televisions and video games. Some people think they need computers and toys.

These things are fun to have. But do we really need them to survive? Of course not!

There are some things we do need. We named some things we don't really need. Now let's figure out what we DO need to survive!

All living things have basic needs. Basic needs are items a living thing requires to survive. If basic needs are not met, the living thing dies.

Basic Needs Must Be Met In Order to Survive

AIR FOOD SUNLIGHT

WATER SPACE SHELTER

Air, food, sunlight, water, space, and shelter are basic needs of living organisms.

BASIC NEWS

Animals need air to breathe. The air must be clean. It must also be the right temperature. Air that is too hot or too cold can hurt an animal.

Animals need clean water to drink. Animals cannot drink salt water. They must drink fresh water.

Animals need food for energy. Energy helps animals move and grow. Some animals eat plants. Some eat other animals. Many animals eat both plants and other animals. What do you like to eat?

Animals need space to live and grow. Some animals live in tiny spaces. Others need more room.

Many animals get fresh water from small ponds and lakes.

Sometimes animals need shelter. Shelter protects animals from bad weather or other animals. Animals can hide in shelter such as forests, rocks, or other structures. Other animals can't find them if they can hide.

The nest is a shelter. It protects the eggs and makes it harder for other animals to find and eat them.

What are the basic needs you can see in the pictures below? Write your answer in the box below each picture.

Accelerate Learning™

try now

Career Corner: Veterinarians

Sometimes animals get sick. One of their basic needs was not met. Maybe an animal is too sick to drink water. Maybe it cannot eat. But with help they can get better.

Veterinarians are animal doctors. They help sick animals get better. Veterinarians take care of many different animals. Some take care of dogs and cats. Others take care of horses and cows.

Plants have basic needs too. Plants need air, water, soil, and space. Plants also need sunlight. They use sunlight, air, and water to make their own food. The air needs to be the right temperature. Some plants can grow in the cold, while others cannot. Other plants like the heat. The amount of water needs to be just right, too.

The veterinarian is taking care of a lizard.

> **nutrient:** a substance that helps a living thing grow and stay healthy

look out!

Both plants and animals need **nutrients**. Animals get nutrients from food. Plants get nutrients from soil.

Look at the plants. Which plant is not getting what it needs? Circle the plant that is not getting what it needs, then write why you know this on the line below.

PLANT A

PLANT B

Plant _____ is not getting what it needs. I know this because

_____.

BASIC NEEDS

Discover Science: Cactus Plants

How do plants survive in the desert? Deserts are very dry. There is not much water. Cactus plants live in deserts. A cactus has thick, waxy leaves. These leaves keep the water inside the cactus. They help the cactus survive.

what do you think? ·

Look at the pictures. Decide if each picture shows a basic need. Write animals, plants, both, or neither. The first one is done.

Hints to help you:

animals – it is a basic need of animals
plants – it is a basic need of plants
both – it is a basic need of animals AND plants
neither – it is NOT a basic need

Sunlight	Water	Shade	Shelter
plants			

Basic Needs on the Go

Most children have a basic understanding of the difference between something they want, and something they need. However, children may assume that items they use every day are essential for life. For example, children may think that cars are a necessity because they are typically used every day. However, they are not considered a basic need.

To help your child understand the difference between a want and a need, find two backpacks or tote bags. Tell your child to pretend the family is going on a backpacking trip in the woods.

In the first bag, the child should add items that support basic needs. This may include bottled water, packaged food, a tent, and similar items. You might want to substitute "pretend" items as needed, such as a sheet in place of a tent and plastic play food in place of real food.

In the second bag, the child should place helpful items that are not basic needs. Items may include a flashlight, a sweater, and a dry pair of socks.

As you place items in their respective bags, discuss with your child:

1. Why is this item a basic need?
2. Why is this item not a basic need?
3. What would you do if you forgot to bring a basic need on the trip?

reflect ·

How do you deal with the cold? Do you walk through snow in sandals? Do you pull on your swimsuit for a nice icy swim? Of course not! People put on their winter coats. Those coats, along with boots, hats, and mittens protect them. People heat their homes in the winter.

Many places get colder in the winter. Other changes happen too. What are they? How do animals and plants survive those changes?

The environment often changes with the seasons. Temperatures get cooler as winter gets closer. Daylight hours get shorter too. Sometimes places get less rain during certain seasons. Plants and animals react to these changes.

Look at the pictures. How are the plants in each season different? What do you think happens to animals that eat plants? Write about it below the pictures.

SPRING

In spring, the plants

_____.

WINTER

In winter, the plants

_____.

Animals that eat plants might need to _____ during the winter.

ENVIRONMENTAL EFFECTS

Some plants go dormant to survive environmental changes. Trees are one example. They go dormant during certain seasons. The trees do not get as much sunlight when days get shorter. They lose their leaves. They slow their growing. They grow new leaves in the spring. These changes happen in winter.

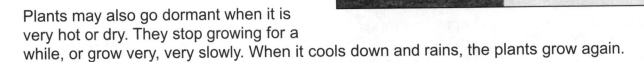

dormant: inactive

Plants may also go dormant when it is very hot or dry. They stop growing for a while, or grow very, very slowly. When it cools down and rains, the plants grow again.

When plants die or go dormant, animals can run out of food. If there is no food, animals might go dormant too. They stop moving around. *Hibernation* is way of going dormant. An animal finds a place to rest. It does not eat. It uses stored energy in its body to survive.

Bats hibernate. They wrap their wings around themselves. They do not move until spring.

Frogs hibernate. This kind digs a hole in soil or in a pile of dead leaves. Some frogs can even freeze solid then thaw out in the spring!

Some animals migrate to survive environmental changes. If the weather changes, some animals leave the area. Some animals fly. Others walk miles and miles. They go to a warmer area during colder seasons. They return in the spring.

This bird migrates from the North Pole to the South Pole. It travels more than 22,000 miles every year!

These animals are called caribou. They migrate each year. They travel up to 3,000 miles.

look out!

Think about how animals might react to cold weather. They don't just react to it by shivering or something similar, they can actually go dormant. Like plants, they can go dormant because of hot temperatures or little rainfall. Others may migrate to cooler places. Some animals migrate when a fire or bad storm kills the plants in the area.

Looking to the Future: Butterfly Migration

Temperatures on Earth change. They go through natural high and low cycles. But many scientists think Earth is slowly getting warmer. This could change animal migration.

For example, monarch butterflies migrate south in the fall. They lay eggs in Mexico. Some years in Mexico have been warmer than others. One day, it might be too warm for the butterflies to lay eggs. The butterflies would have to change their migration pattern to survive. They might have to get there earlier in order to be able to lay eggs.

What if the butterflies could not survive? How might this affect other animals? HINT: Think about other animals that eat butterflies. Write your answer below.

_____

Accelerate Learning™

ENVIRONMENTAL EFFECTS

What Do You Know?

Look at the pictures. Decide how the plants or animals will react to the change. Write HIBERNATE, GO DORMANT, or MIGRATE in the boxes. The first one is done.

Days are getting shorter.

Temperatures are getting cooler.

The trees will likely GO DORMANT.

A fire destroyed most of the plants in the area.

Most of the animals will likely

_____.

There has been very little rainfall.

The corn plants will likely

_____.

It is winter. Most plants are dormant or have died.

Some birds will likely_____.

Go Sky Gazing with Your Child
A great way to teach your child about migration is to look at the skies together during fall or spring and watch for geese or ducks flying overhead. Point out the V formations the birds make, and ask your child to predict why birds make this shape. Then explain that flying in a V formation reduces the wind resistance and keeps the geese from getting tired as quickly as they would otherwise. In other words, the birds do not have as much force pushing against them when they are flying. This saves energy on their long migration. If possible, spend about half an hour watching the skies with your child and counting the numbers of geese you see flying overhead. If making direct observations is not possible (for example, it might be the wrong time of year, or you may live in an urban area), look for pictures of migrating birds in magazines or on the Internet in order to generate a discussion about the V shape.

If time allows, you and your child can do some research on the Internet to find out where the birds are likely going. For example, if you observe Canadian Geese, do a search using "Canadian Geese" and "migration." Keep in mind that websites ending in .gov or .edu are typically more reliable sources of information. Once you have determined the migration route, try to find it on a map, starting with your home location and ending with the birds' final destination.

Here are some questions to discuss with your child:

1. Do you think the birds you observed in the sky or in pictures were migrating north or south? Why?
2. Do all birds migrate? Why or why not?
3. Where would you fly if you were a migrating bird?
4. Do all migrating animals fly? If not, what are some animals that don't fly?

reflect ·

Different plants and animals live together. Look at the picture of the garden. What **organisms** live there? Grass, trees, bugs, and birds live there. Fish and frogs live there, too. Can you think of anything else that might live there?

organism: a living thing

How are these organisms important to one another?

Plants and animals depend on each other in many ways. Bees **pollinate** flowers. Without bees, many flowers could not make more flowers. Other animals need trees for shelter to protect them from weather or other animals. Birds build nests in trees to protect their eggs from predators like snakes. Squirrels use trees to hide their food.

pollinate: the transfer of pollen from one flower to another. This allows flowers to reproduce.

Bees carry pollen from one flower to the next.

The eagles built a nest in the tree.

· ·

Accelerate Learning™

FOOD CHAINS

Animals depend on other organisms for food. Food gives animals energy. All animals need energy to live. Plants need energy too. Where does energy for plants come from? Plants make their own food! But they need a few things to make this food. They make their food using water, air, and sunlight.

Plants are called producers. The word "produce" means "make." A producer is a maker of something. A plant is a maker of food!

Animals can be grouped by what they eat:

- Animals that eat plants are *herbivores*.
- Animals that eat other animals are *carnivores*.
- Animals that eat both plants and animals are *omnivores*.

All organisms die. But what happens then? The plants and animals get broken down into tiny pieces. *Decomposers* do this job. Decomposers live in soil.

Mushrooms are one kind of decomposer.

Accelerate Learning™

Food chains show how food energy moves from one organism to the next. Energy always starts with the Sun. Energy moves from the Sun to producers (the plants). Then it moves from producers to consumers (the animals). Finally, energy moves to decomposers.

Sun $\longrightarrow$ Producer $\longrightarrow$ Consumer $\longrightarrow$ Decomposer

Arrows connect items in a food chain. They show how energy moves.

look out!

Consumers can be herbivores, carnivores, or omnivores. An herbivore always follows a producer in a food chain. A carnivore always follows another consumer. For omnivores, it depends on what they are eating in the food chain.

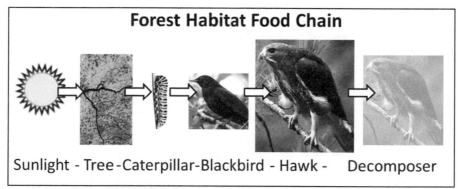

Forest Habitat Food Chain

Sunlight - Tree -Caterpillar-Blackbird - Hawk -   Decomposer

Look at the forest habitat food chain above. Energy starts with the Sun. Write more about the food chain in the blank spaces below.

The _____ is a producer. The _____,

_____, and _____ are consumers.

The caterpillar eats plants. It is a(n) _____.

The blackbird and hawk eat meat. They are _____.

FOOD CHAINS

Food chains are important for life. Imagine if one plant or animal in the chain disappears. Animals further along the chain will suffer. Look at the park **habitat** food chain. What might happen if spiders disappear from the park?

habitat: an area in which organisms live

Park Habitat Food Chain

Sunlight - Oak Tree - Beetle -Spider- Woodpecker- Decomposer

Write your answers below the picture. HINT: What eats spiders?

If spiders disappear from the park, I think _____

_____ because _____

_____.

Accelerate Learning™

What Do You Know?

Look at the beach habitat food chain. Seaweed is a plant-like organism. It uses sunlight to make food. It is a producer. Hermit crabs eat seaweed. Seagulls eat hermit crabs. Sea lions eat seagulls. These organisms are consumers. The hermit crab is an herbivore. The seagull and sea lion are carnivores.

Beach Habitat Food Chain

Sunlight -Seaweed -Hermit - Seagull - Sea Lion - Decomposer
Crab

Now look at the lake food chain below.

- Find the producers and consumers.
- Figure out what eats what.
- Decide whether each consumer is a carnivore or an herbivore.

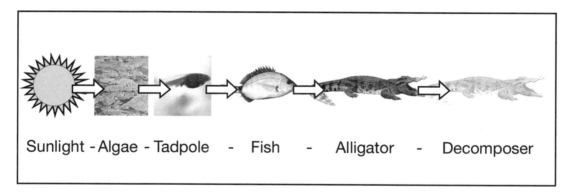

Sunlight - Algae - Tadpole - Fish - Alligator - Decomposer

Write your answers in the chart.

Organism	Producer or Consumer?	If consumer, what does it eat? If producer, leave blank.	If consumer, carnivore or herbivore? If producer, leave blank.
Algae			
Tadpole			
Fish			
Alligator			

Accelerate Learning™

95

FOOD CHAINS

Food Chains at Home

Food chains are a wonderful example of the interdependence of organisms in an environment, and students easily grasp the concept of needing to eat to survive. By discussing how each organism is linked to each other through production, consumption, and decomposition, students gain perspective on the interdependence of living organisms.

One way of discussing food chains is to increase awareness of your child's own place in a food chain. Just before you have your next meal together, grab a sheet of paper and help your child list all of the food items on the plate. Then, after the meal is finished, talk about which food items are producers (all the fruit and vegetables) and which are consumers (any meat products). Some items will be combinations of both. If possible, choose one producer from the list and one consumer, and have your child draw a food chain for each. Arrows should point from the Sun to the producers, then to the consumers. Remind students that in nature, a food chain ends with a decomposer.

For example, if you have a salad as a food item, you might choose lettuce as the producer and your child as the consumer. If you have a hamburger, you might add grass as the producer, then the cow as a consumer, and your child as the next consumer.

Here are some questions to discuss with your child:

1. Are the two food chains you drew the same?

2. Did these foods come from the same type of habitat?

3. What other plants and animals might be part of these food chains?

reflect ·

Do you ever swim underwater? What do you do if you need some air? You come up to the surface. Your lungs help you breathe.

Think about a fish. A fish needs air, too. But a fish can stay underwater and breathe at the same time! What is different about fish that they can breathe under water and we can't?

Fish and humans meet their **basic needs** in different ways. Basic needs include food, air, and water.

What are some other ways animals are different? How do these differences help them meet their needs?

Animals look different from each other. They have different **physical characteristics**. These physical characteristics help animals meet their needs. For example, animals have different body parts that help them move.

Fish have body parts called gills. Gills let fish breathe underwater.

Find the five thin holes on this shark. These cover the gills underneath.

---

basic need: an item a living thing must have in order to stay alive

---

physical characteristic: a feature or trait that can be seen

Fish have fins that help them move and balance in water.

Birds have wings that help them fly.

What is one body part that helps you move? Write your answer below.

_____

ANIMAL CHARACTERISTICS

Animals have different body parts that help them eat.

Elephants have trunks that help them pick up food.

Gophers have paws to help them hold food.

Everyday Life: Human Teeth
Look at your teeth in a mirror. They are different shapes. Why?

Different teeth break down food in different ways. Your front teeth are flat and thin at the bottom. They help cut through food. They can help you take that first bite of a sandwich!

The teeth next to your front teeth are pointed. They tear through food like meat.

Your back teeth are wider. They have bumps that help you grind up and chew food.

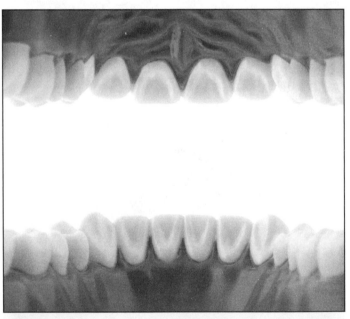

This is a view of human teeth from inside the mouth.

Animals act in different ways. Animals have different **behaviors**. These behaviors help animals meet their needs. Animals can survive because they react and behave in certain ways.

behavior: an action of an animal that can help it stay alive

Lions hunt to meet their need for food. Their claws and teeth help them catch and eat animals.

Seals dive to meet their need for food. Their flippers help them swim through the water.

try now

With a partner, make a list of ways that animals can move. For example:

- Swimming
- Flying
- Crawling

Next, go outside and play a game of tag. For each round, choose a different way of moving from your list. Which movement was the easiest? Which was the hardest? What animals move in these ways?

Draw an animal that hops.	Draw an animal that runs.

Accelerate Learning™

ANIMAL CHARACTERISTICS

We can compare how animals meet their needs. To compare, think about how each bird below looks and acts. Then answer these questions:

- How are they the same?
- How are they different?

Hummingbird

Parrot

Write your answer in the blanks below.

Same: Hummingbirds and parrots both _____.

HINT: What behavior do they use to move?

Different: Hummingbirds have _____ beaks.

             Parrots have _____ beaks.

HINT: How would you describe each bird's beak?

Both birds move by flying. Their wings help them to fly. They fly to find food and water. They also fly to move away from danger.

The birds have different beaks. Hummingbirds' beaks help them reach into flowers for food. Parrots' beaks help them crack hard nuts and seeds.

. . . .

What Do You Know?
Animals have different physical features or traits. They also have different behaviors. Both physical body parts and behaviors help animals meet their basic needs.

Now you try. Look at each animal. Choose a physical characteristic that matches the animal. Then choose a behavior that matches, too. Write your answers to finish the sentences. You will have some leftover words that you don't use.

The crab has large claws to help it grab food.

Physical Characteristics	Behaviors
• strong legs • a long neck • wings • white fur • webbed feet	• swim in water • hide from other animals • eat from trees • jump on land • swing from trees

The giraffe has

_____

to help it

_____

_____ .

The fox has

_____

to help it

_____

_____ .

The frog has

_____

to help it

_____

_____ .

The duck has

_____

to help it

_____

_____ .

ANIMAL CHARACTERISTICS

Observing Animal Characteristics

Take your child to a place where he or she can observe animals. If possible, take your child to the zoo where you will be able to see a wide variety of animals; alternatively, go to a nearby park or pond. You can even observe animals while sitting on a bench in the middle of a city. Bring a notebook so your child can record some observations, either in words or pictures.

Working together, observe how different animals look and act, focusing on one animal at a time. For each animal, help your child sketch and/or write down its physical characteristics (types of body parts, color, etc.) and its behaviors (how it moves, what it eats, etc.) You may wish to ask a zoo or park guide for more information. If you are in an urban setting, look for animals like birds and squirrels.

Once your child has observed and recorded information about several animals, compare how the different animals meet their needs.

Here are some questions to discuss with your child:

1. How do the animals get food and water? (Note that many zoo animals do not have the opportunity to hunt or search for food as they would in the wild, so focus on physical characteristics if you are observing captive animals.)

2. How do the animals move? What body parts help the animals move in this way?

3. In what ways do the animals act like humans do? How are their behaviors different from human behaviors?

reflect ·

Plants are everywhere. People grow them inside. Maybe you have one at home or at school. Think about what it needs. Someone has to water it. It probably needs a special spot in the room, maybe next to a window.

Now think about plants that grow outside. How do they get water? Where do they grow?

Plants have basic needs. A basic need is an item a living thing must have in order to live. Plants need water. They need **nutrients** and air. Plants also need sunlight.

nutrient: a vitamin that helps living things grow

Outside, plants get water when it rains.

Plants get nutrients from soil.

Look at the picture of the plant below. Is it getting what it needs? Circle the answer. How do you know? Write about it below.

The plant IS or IS NOT getting what it needs. I know because …

_____

_____

· ·

PLANT CHARACTERISTICS

Parts of a plant help the plant meet its needs. Roots hold the plant in the soil. Roots also take in water and nutrients from the soil. The stems carry water and nutrients to the rest of the plant. Leaves take in sunlight. Leaves also take in air. The leaves use both sunlight and air to help the plant make its own food. A plant needs food for energy to grow. Flowers hold petals. Petals attract insects. Flowers grow into fruit, which hold the seeds. Seeds grow into new plants.

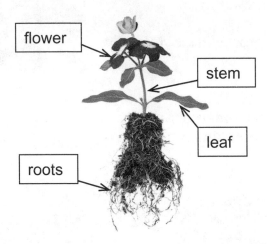

flower

stem

leaf

roots

Label the parts of the plant below.

look out! •

On trees, stems are call trunks. Trees also have branches. They connect to the trunk to the leaves.

This picture is from the bottom of a tree looking up. Can you see the trunk? What about the branches?

Plant parts help plants live in their environments. Plant parts are also called physical characteristics. We can observe these features. Different plants have different physical characteristics. Those characteristics help plants survive in different places.

In dry places, a plant's main root grows very deep. The root can take in water far underground. Plant leaves may also be thicker. Thick leaves help keep water inside the plant.

This type of tree lives in dry places. Its main root can grow over 46 meters underground. That's about 10 times your height!

In wet places, plants do not need deep roots. Water and nutrients are near the top of soil. Some plants get nutrients directly from water.

Water lilies have wide leaves. This helps them float.

Scientists in the Spotlight: Ynes Enriquetta Julietta Mexia
Ynes Enriquetta Julietta Mexia was a scientist. She was from America. Mexia went to school in California when she was 51 years old. She studied botany. Botany is the scientific study of plants.

Mexia became an explorer. She traveled to many places. She collected 145,000 plants. Of those, 500 were plants never found before! Mexia's plant collections can be seen in museums.

PLANT CHARACTERISTICS

What Do You Know?
The parts of a plant help it meet basic needs. Read about each plant. Circle the correct word to complete the sentence. The first one is done.

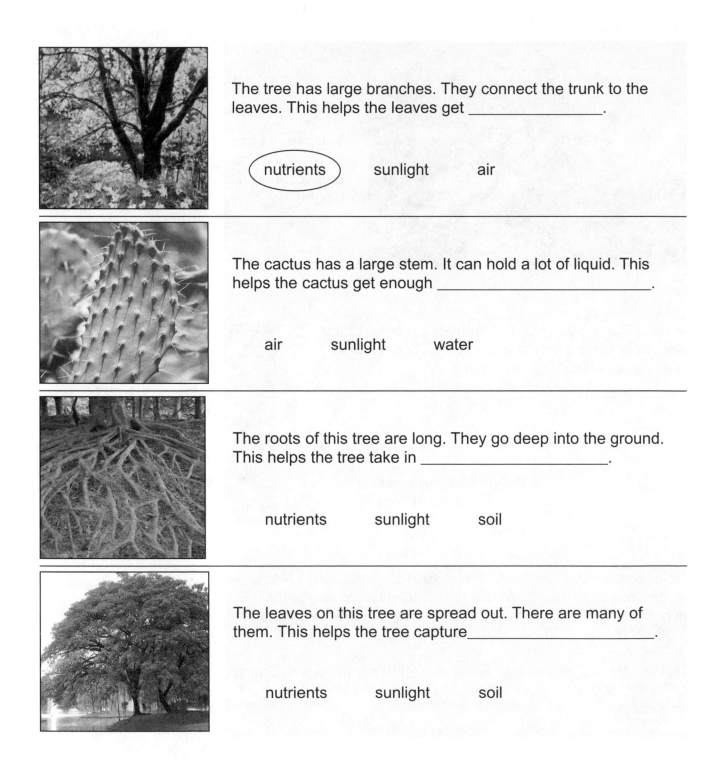

The tree has large branches. They connect the trunk to the leaves. This helps the leaves get _____.

(nutrients)   sunlight   air

The cactus has a large stem. It can hold a lot of liquid. This helps the cactus get enough _____.

air   sunlight   water

The roots of this tree are long. They go deep into the ground. This helps the tree take in _____.

nutrients   sunlight   soil

The leaves on this tree are spread out. There are many of them. This helps the tree capture_____.

nutrients   sunlight   soil

Go on a Plant Hike

To help your child learn more about plant characteristics, take a walk outdoors and search for plants. Look for both small plants, such as ones in pots or gardens, as well as large plants, such as trees. Be sure to point out any plants that are not native to the area and require special care to survive. Discuss with your child what would happen to that plant if a person did not care for it. As you find each plant, discuss the parts of the plant, focusing on the following:

- The roots, which you may not be able to see at all: Point out the kind of soil the plant is in (sandy, clay-like, etc.) and talk about the environment in which you live. For example, if you live in an area with lots of rain, plants you find outside will not require a root structure that is very deep as there is ample water near the surface of the soil. If, however, you live in a dry environment, outdoor plants will need to be drought tolerant or have a deep root structure.

- The stem: Discuss the different kinds of stems—hard or woody stems versus soft stems. Encourage your child to think about the reasons why stems might be different.

- The leaves: Point out differences and similarities in the leaves of the plants that you see. Ask your child to determine whether the leaves are the same thickness. Discuss how the environment in which you live might dictate the types of leaves you are seeing.

Here are some questions to discuss with your child:

1. What is the most likely root structure for plants in your area? Are they long or short? Why?

2. Could a tree grow as tall as it does and live for years if it had a soft stem instead of a hard stem (trunk)?

3. If you keep plants in your home, do the leaves differ from those you see outside? If so, how?

reflect ·

Most animals look like their parents when they are born. The babies are just smaller. They might look like small grown-ups. Kittens look like small cats.

Insects are different. Newborn bees do not look like adult bees. What's going on here? How does the insect change as they grow?

> **insect:** a tiny animal with three body parts, six legs, and antennae; often called a bug

Insects change during their life cycle.

Every living thing has a *life cycle*. It starts when a plant or animal is born. It ends when the plant or animal dies. Life cycles have different stages. *Stages* are times in a living thing's life. For example, you used to be a baby. Now you are a child. These are two different stages in your life. What will happen next? What will you look like when you're an adult?

How are you different now than when you were a baby? Write about two things.

I am different now because

_____

and

_____

Baby is a stage of the human life cycle. What are some other stages?

INSECT LIFE CYCLES

Most insects have four stages. Each stage is different. When you look at an insect you can tell what stage it is in.

The stages of a butterfly

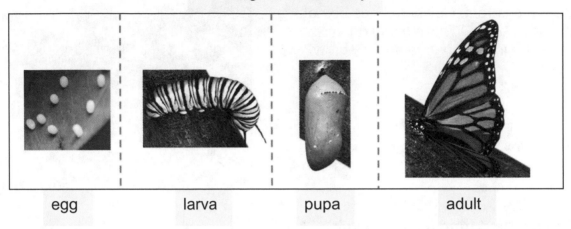

| egg | larva | pupa | adult |

Egg: The first stage is the egg. Adult insects can lay hundreds of eggs. They are very tiny. Sometimes the eggs hatch right away. A mosquito egg hatches in two days! Other eggs survive all winter long before hatching in the spring.

Larva: The next stage is the larva. You might know a caterpillar is a larva! Larvae look like short fat worms with legs. Larvae eat a lot and grow. They shed their skin when they need to grow. Then they grow new skin.

Pupa: After the larva grows enough, insects go into a pupa stage. The larva wraps itself up in a hard shell. This is called a *cocoon* or *chrysalis*. The insect does not come out for a while. It does not eat any food. It rests a lot. But there are big changes happening! Inside, the pupa slowly changes into an adult.

Look closely. You can see butterfly wings inside the chrysalis! The pupa is changing to an adult.

Damselfly larvae live in pond water. Adults live above the water and can fly.

Accelerate Learning™

Adult: The insect comes out of its cocoon as an adult. Adult insects look very different than the larva that entered the cocoon. For example, a wiggly caterpillar enters the pupa stage. But a butterfly that can fly comes out. Many adult insects fly away and lay eggs.

Larva

Adult

(Beetle)

There are many differences between the larva and adult beetle. Name three ways they are different.

1. _____

2. _____

3. _____

try now

Find an insect to observe. You can go outside with an adult. Or you can find a picture of one.

1. If you are outside, use a hand lens to look at the insect. Careful! Do not touch the insect.

2. What stage of the life cycle is it in?

3. How can you tell?

4. Draw a picture of the insect.

Career Corner: Entomologist

Entomologist is a big word. It means a person who studies insects. Entomologists are scientists. They often work outside. They study insect life cycles. They also study how insects act in nature.

Would you like to be an entomologist? Tell why or why not below.

_____

_____

INSECT LIFE CYCLES

What Do You Know?

A cycle is a circle. It always continues. When an insect dies its life cycle ends. But the circle keeps going because adults lay eggs.

You can tell what stage an insect is in by looking at it. The insect here is a larva. It looks like a fat worm. It eats and grows a lot in this stage.

Look at the mosquito life cycle below. Label each stage. Then write one thing you know about that stage.

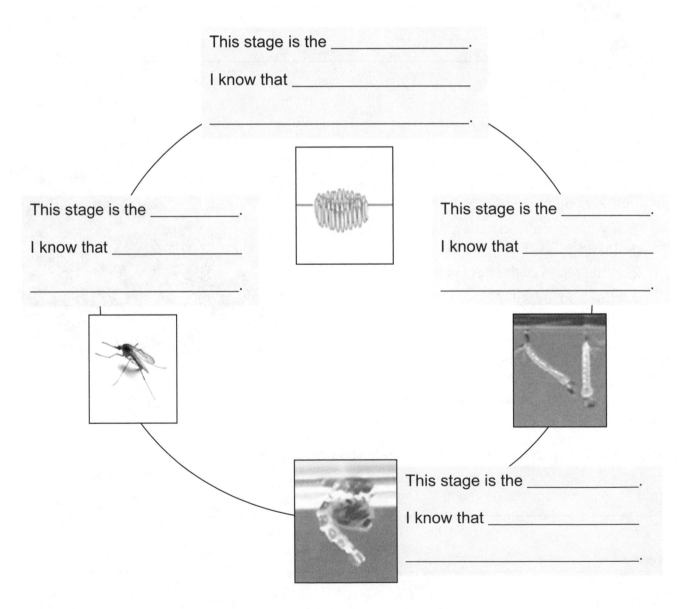

This stage is the _____.

I know that _____

_____.

This stage is the _____.

I know that _____

_____.

This stage is the _____.

I know that _____

_____.

This stage is the _____.

I know that _____

_____.

Observe the Cycle of Life

You can help students understand and observe the changes that take place over an insect's life cycle by researching the life cycle of a ladybug. First, have your child predict, and then describe, what each stage of the ladybug's life cycle will look like. Then, go online (or find some library books) and search for information and pictures of the ladybug life cycle. Focus on learning about some of the behaviors that ladybugs display as they go through each stage.

Next, have your child create a life cycle poster. Print out (or have your child draw) each stage of the ladybug life cycle, and glue the pictures onto poster board to form a "circle of life." Make sure your child draws arrows to connect each stage to the next, and include labels for each stage. Also, have your child write how long each stage typically lasts below each picture.

As an alternate activity, order some insect larvae such as ladybug larvae or caterpillars and raise them in an indoor insect habitat. If you choose this activity, there are many online resources that sell the larvae and the habitats, along with the appropriate food to give the larvae while they are developing. However, please keep in mind that these insects (especially butterflies) should be released into the wild once they reach the adult stage, so you should choose an insect variety that is native to your area. Also consider the time of year—you should not release adult insects during winter if you live in an area that changes dramatically with the seasons.

Here are some questions to discuss with your child:

1. What are the four stages of a ladybug's life cycle?

2. What changes in appearance take place throughout the stages of the life cycle?

3. What changes in behavior take place throughout the stages of the life cycle?

GLOSSARY OF TERMS

Adult – A fully grown insect

Air – The stuff we breathe

Attract – Draw closer to

Basic need – What a living thing must have in order to survive

Behavior – What a plant or animal does

Behavior – The actions of a living thing

Bright – Having a lot of light; opposite of dim

Carnivore – An organism that eats animals

Clouds – A collection of water or ice in the sky

Combine – Mix together

Condensation – Water changing from gas to liquid

Cycle – Something that repeats regularly and never ends

Data – Information that has been collected

Decreasing – Becoming less

Dim – Having only a little light; opposite of bright

Dormancy – Resting for a long time

Egg – The stage where the insect is beginning to form

Electric motor – Machine that uses magnets to help things move; found in many household objects

Energy – What is needed to do work or cause change

Environment – Everything that is around an organism

Evaporation – Water changing from liquid to gas

Flexibility – The ability to bend

Flower – Colorful part of the plant that makes seeds

Food – What plants and animals use for energy

Food chain – The path of energy from one organism to another

Force – What causes things to move

Freeze – When liquids become solids

Geologist – A person who learns about rocks

Growth – Increase

Herbivore – An organism that eats plants

Hibernation – When an animal goes into a deep sleep for a long amount of time

Increasing – Becoming more

Investigate – Try to find answers

GLOSSARY OF TERMS

Lake – Fresh water surrounded by land

Larva – The stage where the insect looks like a worm, has no wings, and is eating a lot

Leaves – Part of the plant that is attached to the step that captures sunlight

Length – How long something is

Life cycles – The stages in an organism's life from birth to death

Light – Energy from the Sun or other source that the eye can see

Liquid – Something that can drip.

Magnet – Piece of metal that attracts objects with iron in them

Manmade – Created or changed by humans

Mass – The amount of stuff in something

Matter – Stuff that everything is made of

Melt – When solids become liquids

Metal – A natural resource found in rocks

Migration – The long distance movement of animals from one place to another

Moon – Object in the sky that changes shape; sometimes it is round and white

Movement – Changing position

Natural – Comes from the Earth

Ocean/sea – Most of the water on Earth; saltwater

Omnivore – An organism that eats both plants and animal

Organism – A plant or animal

Paper – A manmade resource made from wood

Pattern – Something that repeats

Physical characteristic – A feature or trait that can be seen

Physical property – The look, feel, taste, sound, or smell of an object

Plastic – A manmade resource made from oils

Position – Where something is

Precipitation – Rain, snow, sleet, and hail

Precipitation – Water that falls from clouds, such as snow or rain

Predator – An organism that hunts other living things for meat

Predict – To guess before it happens

Prey – An animal that is eaten by another organism

Pupa – The stage where the insect rarely moves because it it growing into an adult

GLOSSARY OF TERMS

Rain gauge – A tool used to measure the amount of rainfall

Repel – Move away from

Resource – Something valuable that we can use

River – Fresh water that flows toward the ocean

Rock or mineral – A piece of the Earth's surface

Root – Part of the plant that holds it in the soil and takes in water

Sanding – To rub away the texture with sandpaper

Soil – Dirt that helps plants grow

Solid – Something we can see that does not drip

Stars – Objects in the sky that you can see shining at night

Stem – Part of the plant that takes the water up to the rest of the plant

Stream – A small freshwater river

Sunlight – The energy from the Sun that plants need to make food

Temperature – How hot or cold something is

Temperature – The amount of heat in an area

Texture – What a surface looks and feels like

Thermometer – A tool used to measure how hot or cold something is

Water – A liquid that all living things need to survive

Weather – What it feels like outside

Wind sock – A tool used to show the direction of the wind

Wood – A natural resource that comes from trees

NOTES

NOTES

NOTES

NOTES

NOTES

NOTES

NOTES

NOTES